Healing TOXIC Habits VOL. 2

Healing TOXIC Habits VOL. 2

MINDSET MATTERS

Presented By
LA'TICIA NICOLE

Published by Publish Your Gift®
An imprint of Purposely Created Publishing Group, LLC

Printed in the United States of America

ISBN: 978-1-64484-560-8 (print)
ISBN: 978-1-64484-597-4 (ebook)

Special discounts are available on bulk quantity purchases by book clubs, associations and special interest groups. For details email: sales@publishyourgift.com or call (888) 949-6228. For information log on to www.PublishYourGift.com

In loving memory of my grandmother,
Inez Laverne Pitts.

I will always love you!

TABLE OF CONTENTS

ACKNOWLEDGMENTS

First and foremost, I would like to thank God who has always been the head of my life. You have been my protector, guidance, safety, help, inspiration, and all that I needed!

To my grandmother, Inez Laverne Pitts, and my grandfather, Eddie Stanton: God said to teach a child in a way they should go, and they won't waver. You both taught me the importance of family and keeping everyone together. I love and miss you very much. I pray I have made you proud.

To my mother, Nora Pitts: You were the first to introduce me to the Lord. I love you for being so strong. Watching you all of my life taught me how to never give up on myself. Thank you, Mommy. I love you!

To my daddy, Gregory Stanton: Thank you for your quiet strength. No one knows your story or would imagine what the Lord has done in our lives. I love you, Daddy!

To my husband, Antonio Beatty: Thank you for never trying to stop or hinder me from pursuing my purpose. I appreciate that very much.

To my two sons, Antonio Carlisle Beatty II and Aden Cole Beatty: You two are my number one reason for going so hard. You are both my reason for staying sane when Mommy wants to fall to pieces at times. I look at your faces, pull myself together, and keep pressing on. Mommy loves you!

To Pastor Rose Thomas and my church family at Unfailing Love Christian Church: Thank you for believing in the God in me.

Thank you to all my friends and family, past radio show guests, listeners, and social media followers. Without you, the vision wouldn't be able to go forth. Thank you for your love and support. Special thanks to my trials and tribulations that birthed #SpeakLife. You didn't kill me. You made me stronger.

FOREWORD

Dr. Portia Lockett

For so long, you have thought there is no hope or that no one else has experienced what you're going through. The spiritual, mental, emotional, physical, and environmental toxins of life were weighing you down. You've been on the brink of giving up and throwing in every last one of your towels that have been saturated with your wailing and tears. Well, the reality is that this book has been divinely written with your trauma and drama in mind by women that have gone through hell, survived, and are now living on the edge of their personal greatness. The collaboration of these authors will compel you to give life another chance. You will be drawn into their testimonies that are shared to inspire and encourage you not to give up.

This is the beginning!
Dr. Portia Lockett

No Longer a Victim

Katrina Bridges

Blessed is the one who perseveres under trial because, having stood the test, that person will receive the crown of life that the Lord has promised to those who love him.
—James 1:12

REPEAT AFTER ME: Love the Lord, stay consistent, see it through!

I've heard people say that our lives are a book and we are the authors. I do believe this is true. However, for many years of my life, I lived with a mentality that led me to believe otherwise and held me back from being who God called me to be. I was not writing the manuscript and taking control of my life. Every family has a unique set of circumstances that make them who they are. Victimizing myself is something I have struggled with almost my entire life. It is something I have seen other people in my family struggle with as well.

From a very young age, I was fearful that my life would be nothing more than the life of anyone who came before me in my family. We didn't have the internet or even cable television when I was growing up. The people I was exposed to in and through my family were all I knew.

I grew up in an unhealthy and unhappy environment. There was domestic violence, poverty, teen pregnancy, an early death rate, mental illness, and drug and alcohol addictions running very deep within my family line. These issues were common amongst almost everyone I saw and everywhere I went. It seemed as if it would take a miracle to work my way out of that lifestyle.

My dad abandoned me and my siblings when I was six years old. My mom struggled as a single parent for most of my life. While I know she tried hard and wanted to make a better life for us, it seemed as if the chains were too strong for her to break on her own while raising us. Sure enough, by the age of thirteen, I was already drinking, using various drugs, and putting myself into some very scary situations for a young girl. This continued for several years. I was right on the path I had always thought I would be on. Fortunately, I got pregnant at a very young age and put an end to that lifestyle, for the most part. I continued the trend of teenage pregnancy that had been prevalent in my family for so many generations prior. While I did an excellent job as a teen mother, I still struggled with feelings of hopelessness. The next phase of my life only made those feelings worse.

I found what I thought was the man of my dreams and had my second child at the age of eighteen. We moved in together and started building a life. I thought I had finally found the peace and stability I so craved. We later had our second child, my third, when I was twenty-five years old. We both worked and tried hard to build a life together. We just could never get it quite right though. After the first few years, our relationship turned very toxic and was riddled with domestic violence. This continued on for eighteen more years. I wasn't allowed to go out and have fun or hang out with friends. Doing pretty much anything outside of my home became a problem for my spouse. I couldn't host family functions at my house or he would be embarrassing, and people would know what an abuser he was. This pushed me to bury myself in work and school as there was nothing else to do. My children were the only good things about the time I spent in that relationship.

When I wasn't working, taking care of kids, or going to school, I drowned myself in unhealthy eating and drinking habits. I overindulged in food and alcohol to the point of reaching almost three hundred pounds. I was depressed, angry, and hopeless. At first, the alcohol was just on the weekends, then it became one during the week, and escalated to where it was almost a nightly occurrence. I was eating fast food and feeling unwell most of the time. I did not have the motivation to take care of my appearance, exercise, or buy new clothes. If I had ever seen a rock bottom, that surely was it. I felt like a failure. I had not yet broken the cycles in my family that I so longed to break. I fought mentally every day. It was a struggle thinking about how I needed to leave the relationship and make a much better life for me and my kids. I knew God called me to be more and do more, but I never could take the plunge and do it.

I victimized myself the entire time and it hindered my ability to see a way out. I did not let myself see past my current situation to a way of life where I was not living every day in survival mode. It was what I was used to, and oddly enough, what seemed normal to me. As I mentioned before, I knew several people who lived in similar situations and died knowing nothing else. Victimizing is so much more than feeling sorry for yourself. When you are constantly making yourself the victim, it's because there is simply too much for you to handle in this world. Too much has been thrown at you and there hasn't been enough time to process it all and heal. It puts a seriously dark cloud over you that seems to follow you everywhere and affects your situations and moods.

I started educating myself on the cycle of domestic violence. I also started keeping a journal on the things that happened, the things that were said, and how I felt. I did that consistently for two years. It was a huge, horrific eye-opener to read. And to think, it was only two years' worth of data from a twenty-year relationship. Keeping a journal is my number one tip for anyone in a domestic violence situation. A lot of people say to do it for evidence, but most people know that will never go anywhere. I recommend keeping a journal because it is so easy to forgive and forget in these situations and the journal doesn't allow you to do that.

I was at a point where I truly did not feel like myself as a person. Dealing with the daily stress of life along with trying to manage the chaos of an abusive relationship became too much for me to handle. I tried everything including counseling, visiting a psychiatrist, and I was even put on medication. All of that did nothing but rake in thousands of dollars in medical bills. Again, I felt hopeless and desperate. I once again turned to my faith and prayed to God for a way out. I will never forget the day that was my final straw. The day I really decided it was over. It was September 7, 2019. We had a gruesome fight that led to me being pulled out of a hiding spot and punched in the forehead. I knew at that moment if I didn't get out of that relationship, it would be the end of me, one way or another.

The victim mentality I carried around for such a long time kept me in bondage. I felt that victimhood was my lot, what I deserved, and how my life was destined to be. Thank God I finally woke up. I had finally had enough. I was tired of letting myself be a victim. I was tired of the shame, guilt, and self-doubt making me wonder if there was ever going to be better in life for me. I was finally ready to leave the relationship and work on creating a better life. I decided my life was going to be worth more and I was going to show my kids what a happy and healthy home looked like. So, with lots of faith and encouragement from special friends, I went for it. I moved away and got a place of my own. I signed the lease on my birthday, which I found to be no coincidence. I had to be willing to go into the unknown, very scared and unsure of what the future held. I knew the whole time though that I was doing what God had been telling me to do for many years.

Unwinding a twenty-year relationship proved to be a very daunting task. I just didn't understand how to let go. I had never let go of anything, good or bad. I had to continually remind myself that settling is sacrificing, and I didn't want to do that anymore. Even though the relationship wasn't healthy, it was still very hard to end. There were so many moments of sadness about the crushed dreams we once shared. One thing a lot of people don't understand about domestic violence is that while you are being hurt or treated poorly, you are still in love. You still love the person and that makes everything that is done to you seem so much worse.

I was moving along nicely, trying to get my kids into a normal routine and starting the repairing of our lives. Then, the COVID-19 pandemic hit. I was already uncertain about my financial future and stressed about all the bills I was now handling on my own, so that led to more fear, loneliness, and worry. Then, my thirty-eight-year-old sister passed away in a tragic car accident leaving behind eight children. Our family was beyond distraught. She was often the glue that held us all together. In search of comfort, those situations almost pushed me back into my old life. But, with God by my side, I stood my ground and stayed strong.

Due to the stay-at-home order put into place in 2020, I was forced to stay home for sixteen weeks straight with all the yuck, guilt, shame, physical pain, and mental strain of my past. Thankfully, the phenomenal company I work for let us all work from home. Without going through the process of fixing myself up, stopping for coffee, driving to the office, going out to lunch, then chitchatting with co-workers during the day, I realized there was a lot more time to think and focus on my life path. As the days in quarantine continued on, I felt the fear my kids were experiencing. They were worried about school and life in general. I had a daughter preparing to go to college and a son who had just started middle school. I tried harder than ever in my life to show up as my best self every day. I wanted them to see that there was still light in this world. I stopped watching the news in my home. Instead, I consistently read and participated in courses for business and personal development.

With my newfound spare time, I focused heavily on inner healing and self-development. At first, I had no clue what that really meant. I had dabbled in it for several years, but never had the time or a peaceful home to really dig into it and stay consistent. I started out doing guided meditations. Some had you visualize walking over a bridge and leaving things in the past. One had you speaking to yourself as a child about how you felt during certain moments of your life. As odd as these activities sound, taking the time to slow your mind down and think about them is a great healing tool that provides so much mental relief. It is almost as intense as the mental satisfaction of getting in a good workout. Meditating, exercising, praying, journaling, and reading the Bible have kept me going. I do all of these regularly now, but before there was never time for any sort of a routine. I try to stay in a mindset of elevated emotion regarding my hopes and dreams. I use affirmations daily. I have a dream book. There are pages and pages filled with my goals and desires. I go into detail on what I want, what it will feel like when I have it, and who I will help along the way. This helps me to stay in an elevated state of emotion regarding my dreams and desires. I also have an app that pops up affirmations on my phone throughout the day. Affirmations are a great tool to use to meditate on a specific phrase. You say that phrase over and over in your mind or write it down. You can post the affirmations in places you look often to help you remember to say them. An example of one I use a lot is, "I deserve to receive all the good life has to offer me." Hire a mentor or latch on to some free resources. There are a plethora of free resources on the internet and on podcasts. Find the tools that work for and benefit you. Keep a log or chart of what you have completed and how it made you feel. Once you find your groove, keep a calendar or a checklist to ensure you are staying consistent with using the tools.

Finding inner healing will help you to trust yourself. When you get to that point, your past will not define you and you will be free to move forward. Learn how to love yourself like you have loved others. There is no time limit that can be put on making yourself feel safe and secure after living in survival mode for years.

I choose to work hard every single day to turn my mindset around. As a result of the work I put in, my life will never be the same. I am still making it a priority to take care of myself mentally and physically. Today, I have so much to celebrate. So many of what I called generational curses on my family have been broken. My kids and I do not look at ourselves as victims. We have our struggles and our issues, but we get up every day and fight for life and what we want out of it. I have a twenty-two-year-old son who is recently married and making well over six figures already. He doesn't have any children yet and is in the process of buying his first home with his wife. I have a daughter who is twenty and away at college working toward a nursing degree. She has broken the cycle of teen pregnancy. Now when I walk into my home, I just look around in amazement that God has blessed my life in such a way and that I have a happy and peaceful home to live in. It is not that it is enormous or expensive, but we are happy, free, and having fun in it. For the first time that I can ever recall, I feel safe and comfortable in my own home.

I've broken the chain of poverty in my family and have a strong six-figure income. In 2020, I grew my side business revenue. New clients and opportunities were practically beating down my door. I believe that was because I was showing up consistently and was confident in my abilities. My mind was free to think about solutions instead of abuse. Throughout 2020 and 2021, I checked off several of the personal and professional goals on my vision board. I wasn't able to focus on my goals as much as I would have liked to while in an abusive relationship because so much of my energy was being consumed. I've successfully lost and kept off over one-hundred pounds for five years. I am working daily to become stronger and healthier, as I had abused my body for so many years. I am no longer taking out my pent-up anger on other people. I am much more pleasant to be around. I've unlearned several bad habits and replaced them with good ones.

I choose to be vulnerable and share my story in hopes that whatever you are going through, you will know it can be overcome. You have a choice. You just have to decide and then see that decision through. Regardless of your current circumstances, always maintain your faith. Put in the work and be prepared for your time to come. Do what you can with what you have. As cliche as it sounds, where there is a will there's a way. You just have to have the courage to see things through. Remember that everything is a result of your actions and thoughts. You are not a victim. When you look at your challenges with this mindset, it's easier to overcome them and make something out of them.

Although I have seen a great deal of turmoil throughout my life, my faith in God has remained steady. I always knew there was a happier life for me. One where I didn't have to be in fight or flight mode on a daily basis. So many of my prayers have been answered. Have your moments, but don't stay there for too long. Pity and the feeling of fighting a storm that will never end can be very daunting, but I assure you there is a way out. I went through one tragedy after another, fighting tooth and nail every day, but now I no longer have to do that. I now believe there are so many possibilities, and the future is bright. I believe I will lead my family into generational wealth and that God is opening doors for us that no one can close. We will continue to break the chains of poverty, domestic violence, teen pregnancy, and mental illness that we know all too well.

Remember, first and foremost, love the Lord; stay consistent; and do what you can, when you can, with what you have at your disposal. Stay prepared and be ready, it will soon be your time.

If you or someone you know is struggling with domestic violence, please reach out to the National Domestic Violence Hotline. You can call, text, or chat with them at https://www.thehotline.org/.

THE NEGATIVE EFFECTS OF SUPPRESSION

La'Ticia Nicole Beatty, RN, BSN, MBA

Refrain from anger and turn from wrath; do not fret—
it leads only to evil.
—Psalm 37:8 (NIV)

REPEAT AFTER ME: I am healed, delivered, and set free from you!

There comes a time when acting like you're healed is not a priority and wanting to be healed, for real, takes over your mind, body, and soul. I feel the need to tell this story now because many of us deal with emotions, specifically anger, and we suppress it instead of allowing ourselves to heal for real. Many times, I thought I was healed from my anger issues, but I was only suppressing them. Suppressing my anger allowed me to feel empowered. I would think to myself, *I did not hit you or run you over or cuss you out or slap you or do something mean back to you so that means I'm in control.* But I found out that while I thought I was in control, I was not. Again, I was suppressing my anger. According to the Cambridge Dictionary, the definition of suppression is the tendency to hold one's anger on the inside without outlet.

I hope this story helps you out because suppressing anger has a negative ending. The truth is, when you hold in your emotions, you build up anxiety. Anxiety can turn into depression and depression can turn into sickness if you do not express how you feel. Many times, I found myself feeling numb, nervous, or stressed out when I wanted to lash out, but did not, at those who had wronged me. That made me feel little, like I was a punk or a peon. I called myself saving them from harm and myself from jail. But, in the end, I was hurting myself because I did not have an outlet for those negative emotions. I was only making matters worse for myself.

There are many verses in the Bible that tell us God will fight our battles, if we would just wait on Him and trust in Him. The Bible also tells us not to fight our own battles, but to give them to God because His yoke is easy and His burden is light. The truth is suppression is not giving your battles to God. Oppression is not giving your battles to God. Regression is not giving your battles to God. I read in the book of Psalms where it states that the Lord is my shepherd, I shall not want. He makes me lie down in green pastures. He leads me beside still waters. He restores my soul. He guides me along the right path for His namesake. And then the Scripture goes on to say that even though I walk through the darkest valley, I will fear no evil for He is with me. The truth is, I have walked through some dark valleys, and I have feared evil because evil had gotten so close to me, I could smell its breath. I realized that I was not truly exercising the Word of God when evil started to manifest in my body.

I do not mean just manifest like a headache. I mean manifest as in, I was experiencing palpitations in my heart, shortness of breath, and sweating profusely from anxiety which can also be called having a panic attack. There have been times when my panic attacks were so bad that I thought I had a heart attack. Those panic attacks came from regression and suppressing my emotions instead of talking them out. I did not understand at the time that I needed an outlet from all of the things that were irritating me. The things that I kept hidden in my mind. The thoughts that I did not want to bring out to hurt other people. But I needed an outlet, somewhere, somehow. I had no idea that I was hurting myself by suppressing my emotions. I thought that if I did not hurt anyone else, if I did not lash out, if I did not tell anybody's business, if I just kept all that emotion to myself that I was doing the right thing. But the truth of the matter is, I was always hurting myself while trying to protect other people. The truth of the matter is, I should have spoken to somebody—a psychiatrist or even a counselor or my pastor. I should have talked to somebody, but I allowed suppression to push me into a place called depression.

According to the Oxford English Dictionary, depression is a medical condition in which a person feels very sad and anxious and often has physical symptoms, such as being unable to sleep. Well, what I learned is that when I went into depression, regression was right around the corner. I ended up back where I started. The definition of regression, according to the Oxford English Dictionary, is a return to a formal or less developed state. I found myself in that formal and less developed state. I went back to my old ways. I was not healed of past trauma. I was fighting depression, which led to regression. I remember times when I got very mad at people who were trying to bully me on social media. I felt like if I ever saw them, I would hurt them badly. And instead of taking my anger to God, I let it build up. I told myself, *They are not bothering me, as long as they don't touch me. They are not bothering me, if they're not saying it to my face. I don't have a problem with them. As long as they don't come to me, I don't really care what they do.* The truth was they were being disrespectful, and I wanted to hurt them. I did not take it to God in prayer. I kept telling myself, *I'm being persecuted for His namesake.* However, what I did not do was acknowledge how their bullying made me feel. It took me a long time to acknowledge how being raped made me feel, how being molested made me feel, how being urinated on by my babysitters' brother made me feel, how being rejected made me feel. I had not gotten to a point where I could acknowledge how being disrespected made me feel.

I understand if you're reading this and saying to yourself, "Not Minister Beatty. You ain't nobody. People are disrespecting Jesus, so they are going to disrespect you." I understand what you are saying because I say that all the time. People disrespected Jesus. But the truth of the matter is, we are still human and when people disrespect you, it makes you feel a certain kind of way. That is when you should acknowledge your feelings. The Word of God tells us to have no anxiety but in everything by prayer and supplication with thanksgiving let our request be made known unto God. The Lord is telling us to cry out to Him. He will hear us, and He is going to deliver us. Unfortunately, when we don't listen to the Word of God and take things into our own hands, we bring on consequences such as sickness in our minds, bodies, and souls. This happens when we do not acknowledge our true feelings. We open the door for more spirits to come in.

When the spirits come in, they do not just come by themselves, they bring seven more spirits. It tells us in Matthew 12:43-45 (NIV), "When an impure spirit comes out of a person, it goes through arid places seeking rest and does not find it. Then it says, 'I will return to the house I left.' When it arrives, it finds the house unoccupied, swept clean and put in order. Then it goes and takes with it seven other spirits more wicked than itself, and they go in and live there. And the final condition of that person is worse than the first. That is how it will be with this wicked generation."

When I read that Scripture, I realized that when we suppress our emotions and we don't get true deliverance from God, impostor syndrome and false humility creeps in. We are not being healed, delivered, and set free. We become worse. In other words, if you clean your mind, body, and soul but you do not fill it with the Word of God, spirits come back, bringing seven more spirits with them. I remember feeling like I was living for God because I thought that I cleaned every window, door, drawer, and closet in the house. However, I did not fill it back up with the Word of God and I found myself worse off than before. I felt like I was doing the right things to heal, but again, I was in denial.

There I was pacing around my empty house. My husband and I were separated. It was his turn to have the children that weekend and I was left feeling alone and confused. I remember it like it was yesterday. I was crying and pacing back and forth, speaking negatively to myself. It was like the enemy was putting words in my mind and they came right out of my mouth. Before I knew it, I had my 380 pistol in my right hand. I took off the safety and turned my laser on. I then began to cry even harder as I talked to myself, trying to convince myself to pull the trigger. I could hear myself saying, "The boys don't need you; they have their dad and family here. Nobody loves you; nobody likes you. Pull the trigger. Pull the trigger." Unexpectedly, my cat, Dora, started jumping up on the walls and running in a circle around me. For one second, I was able to snap out of that horrible place and say, "What are you doing, Dora?" She was probably thinking to herself, *What are you doing, Momma?* Dora was chasing the laser of the gun. She was playing with the little red light. Praise God for Dora. She stopped me from those negative thoughts. I then started to play with her using the laser, having her run in circles and up the wall. Then, I put my gun in my side drawer, laid down, and went to sleep. When I woke up, I happened to see a mirror on my dresser. I picked it up and began to speak life into myself. I told myself that I was worth living for. I am loved. I am beautiful, I am blessed, and I can do all things through Christ that gives me strength.

Speaking life became a habit for me. Every morning, I found myself using social media to do it. When I saw that my words were not only helping me but helping others, I vowed to myself to speak my truth even if it makes me look crazy to others. I cannot be in a prison while others appear to be free. So, I have learned to take things to God in prayer and allow the process of healing to take place. Now, I am not sitting here telling you that I have it all together. There are times when I still find myself fighting internally to speak up for myself. I have lost some relationships that I gained over the years because the person they met was so passive and was not speaking up. So now, when I do not allow people to run over me or to say anything to me and I speak up for myself, they disappear. I am okay with that.

I will no longer allow people to bully me out of my purpose. I will no longer allow people into my heart, head, or life (and some were in my pocket) that do not belong there. I know that I am a good person, friend, sister, wife, and mother. I am not perfect, but I am good. So, when bad things happen, I know they were meant for evil, but they always turn out for my good.

When dealing with depression, regression, and suppression, know that there will always be a battle. What I want you to learn from this chapter of healing is that once you identify your toxic habits, there are Scriptures, affirmations, and books that will help you change your thoughts, which could change your life. According to 2 Timothy 1:7 (KJV), "For God hath not given us the spirit of fear; but of power, and of love, and of a sound mind." Knowing this, I was able to identify my toxic habits and work on myself using the Word of God. The Word tells us that we should not just be hearers of the Word, but we should be doers of it because, if we aren't, we only deceive ourselves. Though this fight may look to others as being hypocritical because you are constantly warring with yourself, be the best you can be. Make sure that you continue to not only read the Word of God, but believe it for yourself, then apply it. There will be times when you find yourself feeling up and there will be times when you find yourself feeling down. Just know the times that you find yourself feeling down are when you can look up to the hills from which come your help, according to the Word of God. In this journey called life, I realized that my help only comes from God. People come and go, but God never changes. He has remained the same.

In conclusion, after identifying my toxic habit of suppression which led to regression, I encourage you to assess your own life. First, after the initial assessment and finding where you have exhibited toxic habits, make a plan to apply the Word of God. Second, implement what you have learned from the Word. Third, evaluate how your toxic habits make you feel. Fourth, continue to execute what makes you the best you that you can be.

This system of implementing and changing will be an ongoing process throughout your life. We are always changing; things are never the same. So, make sure you assess where you are then plan, evaluate, and execute your plan. You can do it. I believe in you.

THE WOUNDED HEALER

Trish Noel

*He gives strength to the weary and increases the
power of the weak.*

*Even youths grow tired and weary, and young men
stumble and fall;*

but those who hope in the Lord will renew their strength.

*They will soar on wings like eagles; they will run and not
grow weary, they will walk and not be faint.*
—Romans 40:29-31

**REPEAT AFTER ME: The fire will not consume you, but
instead, you shall come forth like pure gold.**

Walk with me on this journey. You are at your favorite music concert. The music is pumping. The crowd is hyped. You are with perfect company. Right vibe. Right mood. Perfect ambiance. Life is great!

You are a lover of live music. You are living in the moment—grooving with the band and clapping, screaming, dancing. Everything that comes with the right groove. You are singing along and feeling the vibrations of the bass guitar. Man, things cannot get any better. This is the life!

Suddenly, you begin to feel overheated. The room starts to close in on you. The music, the people, the sounds become muffled. You think to yourself, *If I can get to a cool place, I will be okay.* Over the loud sound of the band, you whisper to your friend, "I'm going to the restroom. I'll be right back." You are not saying how you feel.

You move slowly through the crowd. Purposeful. Intentional. You are trying not to over-exert yourself. The crowd appears to be closing in on you. You are squeezing past people and focusing on your current mission. You need to get to the restroom. People are everywhere, bumping into you as they continue to enjoy the concert. How would they know you are in the midst of a crisis? Yet, you are focused. You are trying not to succumb to the feeling of panic.

You observe your surroundings. How much farther do I have to go? The walls are steadily closing in on you. You keep telling yourself, *You're gonna be okay. Just take your time. Don't panic. Breathe. Walk. Breathe. Walk. You're almost there. C'mon girl. You got this!*

As you get closer to the restroom, you begin to feel yourself fading. Your inner being shouts, *Don't do it!! Go! You're almost there! Just get into a stall! Just get into a stall! You'll be okay! You got this!* Outside of the restroom is a small floral décor sitting on a table. It's only about six feet in front of you, but it seems like it is miles away. You set your sight on the floral décor, thinking, *You're almost there. C'mon, you got this! Don't lose it!*

You see the floral décor. It's almost within reach. Yes, you're almost there. Just keep moving. As you get closer to the floral arrangement, you begin to feel the coolness of the air conditioner flowing from the restroom. In your mind, you're saying to yourself, *Yes, finally, I'm here.* Yet, you feel yourself steadily fading. Your only goal now is getting into the stall before passing out. Holding on with everything you've got, you start talking to yourself again, *You're going to be alright. You're almost there. Hold on!*

What do you do when all you can do is hold on? Hold on!

The crazy part of all of this is that I am very much aware of my surroundings. However, I have no control over what is going on within my body. Things begin to happen to my body. I begin to experience cold sweats. I feel the sweat rolling down my arm and my back and beading across my forehead. My skin becomes cold and clammy. It is wet and sticky to the touch. My heart is racing. Imagine the scene in the movie *Get Out*. I'm in the "sunken place." I am aware, yet I'm falling with no control. I am unsuccessfully trying to grasp reality. What is happening? Why now? I am doing all I can to calm down. Epic fail!

Finally, I make it to the restroom. I feel like I have been on a five-mile hike in the scorching heat with no water, nothing to hydrate or revitalize myself. I see the stall. Now, to just walk into it slowly, cautiously, intentionally. I can see the restroom attendant. She greets me. I return the greeting. There is no one in the restroom but the two of us. Walk! No time for conversation. I am still fading! I enter the first stall. *Yes!* I'm here. I am feeling the coldness of the air conditioner. *Lord, thank You,* I say to myself. I close the door and rest my head against the cold wall. Now, to just sit down. C'mon girl. You're almost there.

I back up to sit on the toilet seat while telling myself, *Just sit there! Be still. Breathe. It will be over in a few minutes.* I hear the restroom attendant ask, "Are you okay?" I respond, "Yes, Ma'am." But am I? I reach behind me. I can feel the seat. Sit down!! I go to sit down, and my tailbone hits the front of the toilet. BAM! I hit the floor. I hear the attendant, "Ma'am, are you okay?" "Yes," I respond. I am, now. The floor is cold and just what I needed. Again, I am aware of my surroundings, yet, I cannot physically respond to anything. Verbally, I can answer, but I cannot reach the lock to unlock the door. She opens the door. I hear her call for help.

"I'm okay," I tell her. "Please give me a cold towel. I just need a minute." She wets a towel and places it on my forehead. Within a few minutes, I'm beginning to feel normal, whatever normal is. I am still lying on the floor, as it feels like Heaven. I hear my friend in the background calling my name. They let her in. She knew the commotion was over me. I'm okay now. Can I just go home? No, I must go to the hospital to be evaluated, since I fell, according to the venue's policy. It felt like the paramedics were standing outside the restroom door. How did they get here so quickly? Were they there all along? Lifting and strapping me in, they continue checking my vitals and my head and neck for injuries. Vitals are stable. Tailbone decides it wants to feel pain. I am exhausted from the experience. Off to the nearest hospital with my friend following behind.

What an event. Have you ever experienced anything like that? What is wrong with me? Why does this continue to happen? After being in the hospital for two days, the diagnosis was vasovagal syncope. What? Vasovagal syncope. A sudden drop in heart rate and blood pressure leading to fainting, often in reaction to a stressful trigger. What stressful trigger did I experience? I was at a concert! I was enjoying my evening. I was not stressed.

As we reviewed my medical history, I realized I had experienced these episodes multiple times in the past but not to this degree. I researched the diagnosis, learning that vasovagal syncope can be caused by somatization disorder, anxiety, depression, and panic. The response involves the central nervous system (brain and spine), cardiovascular system (blood vessels and heart), and the peripheral system (nerves). This was all new to me. However, I could finally put a name to what I was experiencing. Now what?

Stress. Anxiety. Depression. Common words known and experienced by many. As a mental health professional, these terms were all too familiar to me. As a mental health professional, why was I experiencing these things? My life should be together. I trained for this profession to help people who experience mental illnesses. Surely, not I.

Throughout my life, I had to learn to manage *my* stress. Everyone experiences stress. Right? Stress is common. However, my stress began to manifest into anxiety. I was becoming anxious about everything—the unexpected, the what-ifs, and everything that comes with it. This was my "new normal."

There were so many things I wanted to accomplish in my life, but my anxiety was getting in the way. Where did it all begin? I spent years trying to find the source, yet still do not know. I recalled events, like what happened at the concert, which exacerbated my anxiety. I remembered an episode while riding on a bus traveling to Baltimore. Another episode on a Thanksgiving Day which landed me in the hospital once again. Where did this all come from? I had gotten used to hiding it and keeping it to myself; now it was rearing its ugly head in public for all to see. I needed to gain control over it.

Wounded healer is a term used in the mental health profession to describe those who work in this field who have their own personal wounds. Yet, despite their wounds, they are able to help others heal. I was truly the wounded healer. I had to embrace my own wounds and my own mental health. It was hard to admit that I struggled with anxiety. I am supposed to have this perfect, professional life. I am a helper. I have always helped people. I am the one who is supposed to have it together. So, why am I struggling with anxiety? Who is this woman?

In 2010, my family and I relocated from Baltimore, Maryland, to Durham, North Carolina. I was headed for a fresh start. Finally, life was going to be different. It was going to be great. I prayed. I asked God to shake things up in my life, in my marriage. Things had to get better. Something needed to change. Well, life in the Carolinas brought about a different set of challenges. I have heard people say, be careful what you pray for. In my mind, I had this plan for what I wanted God to do. Oh, but God. He said, "I have *my* own plan for you, my child." So, beware, the answer to your prayer may not come the way you expect.

A year after relocating, my husband and I separated. The bubble that protected our marriage was now gone, and we had to face our truths on our own. It was hard but necessary. No more existing in a relationship that we both knew needed to change. Many asked, "What happened? You guys were the perfect couple." Little did they know that we were hurting inside, existing in our marriage and our lives but not living. We served in our church and in our community. We were existing in this life God had given us. We had lost sight of serving one another.

Separation brought about many emotions. I struggled with how I was going to survive. What would happen to our children? I felt shame, doubt, fear, and most of all, this thing called anxiety was at full force. I had become anxious about everything, but I was good at hiding my anxiety. No one could know. I had to control it. It could not get the best of me. Yet, the more I felt like *I* was controlling it, *it* was controlling me.

I was overcome with guilt, as my two younger children would cry at night, wanting their family to be whole again. However, I knew I couldn't go back. I saw myself become someone I did not know. I was short with my children. I did not want to deal with people. I had no patience for anything or anybody. I lacked energy. My health issues were becoming exacerbated. I suffered from chronic pain and had to learn how to manage it, as it affected my daily living. I was taking thirteen pain medications a day to survive. I was already overweight and gaining more weight. It was too painful, physically, to get out of bed. It was a struggle functioning at work with the amount of medication I was taking daily. Depression was creeping in, and there was nothing I could do about it. On the outside, it appeared as if I had it all together but, on the inside, I was drowning.

Every night, after my children fell asleep, I would find myself crying for God to please help me. What was I to do? I asked Him to show me. I decided to find a therapist for my children, as they needed someone besides me to help them with their emotions. But what about me? Well, I am a mental health professional. Why not seek mental health treatment? My emotions were running rampant. Finally, I decided to stop giving into shame and guilt and seek therapy myself. Therapy was one of the hardest things I had to do but one of the most rewarding things I did for myself. It was time for self-healing. I was referred to a faith-based therapist who helped me on the journey of changing my life.

The shame was real! I'm a therapist, so why was I ashamed to see a therapist? The wounded healer needs healing too. No one could fix my life but me and God. I had to work through not worrying about what people would say or think. This was my life, and I wanted to live it in a healthy, happy, and productive way. I still had dreams that I wanted to achieve. There was still life to live, but I needed to find myself first.

Therapy meant I had to start taking responsibility for the toxic habits I had developed. I had to take responsibility for the role I played in the dissolution of my marriage. And I had to learn to say "no." Saying "no" is not selfish, even though some may not like it. I must do what is best for me. However, all of this was extremely hard, as I had to admit some truths to myself. I had to do some deep soul searching to begin to heal and feel whole again. The process took time, work, and gut-wrenching honesty with myself. It also took forgiveness. I had to learn to forgive others, ask for forgiveness, and most importantly, forgive myself.

I was in therapy once a week, then we met biweekly. During therapy, I was challenged to make entries into a gratitude journal. I had to write three things I was grateful for daily. That allowed me to focus on the positive things in my life and not so much on the negative. Wow, I had lost sight of the joys in my life. I had always journaled, but I began to take my daily journaling more seriously. I had my gratitude journal and my daily journal which included Scriptures, prayers, goals, dreams, and outrageous things that I knew would only come from God. There were days when I may have just entered a Scripture or a word, and then there were days when I would write pages and pages of thoughts, fears, accomplishments, whatever was in my heart and on my mind. I was beginning to heal. I externalized on paper everything that I was feeling or thinking. I no longer kept things in my head or my heart; I got them out. I was learning to put myself first and not worry about what people may say or think because I can only control myself. And to be honest, people will talk about you whether you are doing good or bad, so live your life according to your authentic self and God's will.

It took four years of therapy to work through that phase of my life. I'm still working on it, but my life has changed drastically. Yes, I still deal with anxiety but not depression. I still seek therapy and even medication management to deal with my anxiety, as sometimes life can be overwhelming, but that is okay! Now, I look at life through a different lens.

Recently, my family experienced a house fire. It was devastating. I was devastated. I felt so much guilt, fear, and a sense of hopelessness like never before. I kept thinking, *God, I've come so far, now this. What are you trying to show me* now? The new lesson I learned was how to receive and ask for help. I felt guilty receiving help, and to be honest, I felt ashamed. It was okay for people to know we had a fire, but it was not okay for people to help us recover from the fire. Many conversations were had with old and new friends about receiving help. It was a struggle. I was focused so much on myself and my feelings that I forgot I had a family, and we genuinely needed help. We received an outpouring of love and support from family, friends, and strangers. It was amazing, and God showed me that it was okay to accept and even ask for help, as people wanted to help and were generous in their support. I learned and am still learning from that experience. It is okay to ask for help. It is okay to receive help.

When I think about my life, I think of the phoenix. In Greek mythology, the phoenix is described as a large bird. It is larger than an eagle and has beautiful, colorful feathers. The myth states that the phoenix lives for five hundred years. It builds a nest of spices and aromatic plants, striking its beak against a rock for a spark. It then flaps its wings, setting the nest and itself on fire. As the phoenix dies, a new one is born. The phoenix represents birth, death, and rebirth. The legend of the phoenix states that its ashes can bring life to the dead, and its tears can heal whatever it touches. What a powerful bird!

I have been through the fire. Figuratively and literally. I had lost sight of life and who I was as a person. I had grown tired and weary. I felt like giving up many times. But I could not because I had a family. I have cried myself to sleep many nights. I have cried out to God to get me through, as I knew not what to do. I felt lost and hopeless. I stumbled and fell many times, but I kept getting back up. Through the grace of God, the one true thing that remained constant in my life was my relationship with Him. Even when I stumbled and fell, He was still there to catch me. He gave me strength when I did not know how I was going to make it. He increased my power to want to live, to want to fight, to hold on to that *hope* in Him as I go through the rebirthing stage. Like the phoenix, I experienced birth and death. Now, I am going through a rebirth.

It took for me to come of age before I understood who I was and who I am. I had to stop, reflect, and be honest with myself about who I thought I was and who I truly am. Transparency is scary. Being truthful with yourself means digging deep—looking at the good, the bad, and the ugly—and not being ashamed of what people may think. When I was approached about becoming a contributing author of this book, I was excited. However, the more we met and discussed what the book entailed, hesitancy kicked in. I thought to myself, *Is this something I sincerely want to do? Am I ready to be open with the world about my life?* Well, here I am!

Who am I? I was a wife for twenty-eight years. And I have been a mom, a daughter, a sister, a cousin, a friend, and a confidant for so long that I forgot who I was. I am now a divorced mom of three adult children. Wow! I called them adults. I am a caregiver of an aging parent. I am a mental health professional. I am an entrepreneur. I am a woman who is a giver, helper, nurturer, and listener by nature. I am a woman who struggles with asking for and receiving help. I am a woman who continues to learn how to say "no." I am a woman who is taking responsibility for her life choices. I am a woman with an anxiety disorder. I have not arrived, but I am a far cry from where I used to be. With God, many prayers, therapy, and medication (it all works hand in hand), I am a woman who the fires of life will not consume. I shall come forth as pure gold. I am where I am because of God, and to God be the glory.

Relentless Abundance

Yolanda Spearman

"'If you can'?" said Jesus. 'Everything is possible
for one who believes.'"
—Mark 9:23 (NIV)

REPEAT AFTER ME: I believe all things are possible.

After about six months of marriage, at age thirty-five, I woke my husband up in the middle of the night, declaring that I had a special dream. I shook him awake, eagerly exclaiming, "Mark, I had a dream that we are going to have a baby girl named Zoe. I feel like this is a message from God preparing us for our future." My husband rolled over, looked at me like I was crazy, and went right back to sleep.

I never imagined the impact that vision would have on my life. That dream became a nightmare before it became a blessing. I thought pregnancy would come naturally. People all around me popped up pregnant every day. My nieces and nephews shot out one after another at what seemed like an alarming rate, yet I was childless.

This is me, unedited. Yolanda Spearman. Author, teacher, corporate professional, relentless dreamer, and pursuer of more.

When I turned thirty-eight and still didn't have any children, I felt sorely disappointed. I believed with all my heart that the dream I had was from God, and I could not understand why I didn't get pregnant. I drowned my sorrows in solitude and lifted my spirits by being the favorite aunt. It became a tradition to take my nieces and nephew to see every kid's movie as soon as it came out. We enjoyed many fun playdates, and I pretended that they were my kids.

The Bible says in Proverbs 13:12 that "hope deferred makes the heart sick," and oh, was my heart sick. I went to see an infertility doctor, and the journey of 1,820 days began. I experienced every treatment known at the time including fibroid surgery, clomid, artificial insemination, in vitro fertilization (IVF), IVF with intracytoplasmic sperm injection, frozen embryo transfers, fertility acupuncture, fertility massages, and other holistic treatments. I did it all again and again and again until "no" became an echo that haunted my dreams. I heard "no" so often that I was certain I missed the message of that dream I had long ago, the one about my daughter Zoe.

After five years of trying, sex became a science experiment in my house. My heart and mind were consumed with the desperate need to be a mother. All I talked about was having a baby. My husband tired of going into the fertility office to make sperm deposits, and he felt annoyed at me for being sad all the time.

My toxic habit was focusing on *lack* instead of focusing on *abundance*. I constantly spent time basking in the challenges of my situation. Then one day, I decided to believe God. John 10:10 says, "The thief comes to steal, kill, and destroy" and my focus on lack stole my joy, killed my hope, and was destroying my marriage. When I shifted my focus to the second part of the Scripture which says, "But I have come that they might have life and have it more abundantly," my perspective changed. I went from asking God, "Why me?" to thanking Him for all that He had already given me. I made a courageous decision to stop trying to get pregnant. First, I told my husband, through tears and a lot of tissue, that I was happy with our life and I was willing to work to save our marriage. Then, I went to my fertility doctor for one last visit. The nurses knew me so well they acted like family. I brought them their favorite snacks because I visited the office frequently. On that visit, I brought in Timbits, a favorite passion of the nurses. Those tiny donut holes set the foundation for my declaration. As we munched and chatted away about life, I casually mentioned that my journey to motherhood had reached the end. A nurse burst into tears, and of course, I did too. She lamented with me and urged me to try one last time before throwing in the towel.

Unbeknownst to me, my insurance policy carried a special fertility rider that provided me with a huge policy benefit. And after my many attempts, just enough remained for one last attempt. I agreed.

As we discussed the final attempt, the nurse begged the doctor to break her standard, conservative IVF protocol. Normally, the doctor would only insert three fertilized eggs, based on my age and a host of other rules. After the nurse intervened on my behalf, much to the annoyance of the doctor, she relented and agreed to insert four eggs instead of three. The doctor did not do that easily. She made me sign a document that I would abort two of the fetuses if I got pregnant with quadruplets. I agreed because I wasn't going to say a word to cause her to change her mind.

I got pregnant with three of the four eggs. I am from Michigan, and I traveled to a training event in Texas for work. Just before the event began, I started bleeding profusely. I was scheduled to conduct the class. No one knew that I was pregnant, so embarrassingly I had to confide in one of the organizers of the session. Due to the severity of the bleeding, she drove me to the emergency room. After a long wait, the doctor entered the waiting area, shaking her head sadly. She said that two of the embryos didn't survive. She acted somber, but I smiled because I had changed my toxic habit of focusing on *lack* to focusing on *abundance*. I told the doctor I was committed to channeling positivity not negativity to my baby. I believed the one that survived was the girl in my dreams, Zoe. I kept the faith that the little girl from that dream was in a fight for her life and I was committed to helping her get here. When I flew back to Michigan, my doctor joined the fight with me. Her name is Dr. Jennifer Kaplan. I lovingly call her Dr. K.

Dr. K. knew all about my dream, from five years prior, of having a baby girl named Zoe. She doted on me. I think she felt sorry for me, but she played along with a game face. Because I believed my pregnancy was a miracle, I told Dr. K. that I didn't want to know the baby's gender.

I forgot to mention that I was almost forty years old at the time, which is considered a geriatric pregnancy in baby birthing terms. That meant that the likelihood of problems was excessively high. Basically, the odds were against me. But my mother kept reminding me of Romans 8:31 which says, "If God be for us who in the world can be against us," and Isaiah 41:10 which says, "Do not fear for I am with you, I am your God. I will strengthen you."

Then, the worst happened. I was diagnosed with an incompetent cervix and put on bed rest. I had to lie flat on my back in the hospital for three months and ten days. My hopes wavered. It was my family that helped me keep the faith. My sister bought a tiny little four-leaf clover and hung it up on the bathroom door so that I could visualize *life*.

When I took my eyes off my circumstances and focused on my efforts to improve my situation, I realized how faith becomes an action word. What do I mean by that? I mean, when we allow self-denigrating thoughts to come in, they destroy our soul. Our spirit craves inspiration, and to move forward we must provide the source of that inspiration by healing toxic habits.

Healing the Toxic Habit

Action one: Sometimes you need a faith extender, which is something that will remind you to stay focused on the end goal and push away distractions.

My mother prayed and made me confess Ephesians 3:20, "Now to him who is able to do immeasurably more than all that we ask or imagine, according to his power that is at work within us."

Action two: Surround yourself with people who speak life.

I believed that I was having a girl named Zoe because I saw her in a dream. The dream felt like God speaking to me personally. And while I wanted to believe God, at the same time, the doctors kept preparing me to face the facts that my body was rejecting the pregnancy and I would likely lose the baby.

Yet, I kept the faith. I wouldn't allow the doctors to tell me the sex of the baby. All of this happened before gender reveals were popular. I found out the gender two-weeks before the baby was born. At week thirty, the little miracle—Zoe Spearman—was born at four pounds, six ounces. Before her birth, I wondered about the significance of the name Zoe (pronounced Zoey). I researched it a bit while lying in my hospital bed and discovered that in Greek her name means "the life of God." I carried the life of God from a dream to reality.

I released my focus on *lack* and shifted into *abundance*. Once I shifted my energy, I created an environment that could sustain life.

Would you believe that I did this entire process one more time? I decided that I didn't want Zoe to be alone. There were no visions involved this time around. I wanted my daughter to have a sibling. My poor husband objected feverishly and would only allow me to try with one egg. I have to tell you, I almost divorced his butt over it. It took four eggs to get one baby, and now he wanted me to try with just one egg. I was angry, but I did it. And it worked. I got a beautiful, healthy baby boy named Marcus Spearman. He is just as much of a miracle as Zoe because I was in the hospital on bed rest while pregnant with him for twenty-seven weeks, and every doctor expected him to be a preemie because by that time I was forty-one. The doctor came to visit me one day and offered me the services of a psychiatrist because I refused to focus on *lack*. I spoke over my son that he would have life and have it more abundantly. I even bet the doctor that my son would be healthy. And I declared that when he was born healthy, I would come back to the office, find her, and tell her, "I told you so."

Action three: You can't just talk about what you are doing differently. Bold faith takes bold actions.

My son, Marcus, stayed in my womb until week thirty-eight. He was born healthy and strong with no issues. I went back to that office, I found that doctor, and I said, "I told you so."

Here is my point. Our dreams don't always manifest the way we think they will, and sometimes toxic habits can and will creep back into our lives. We must exercise fortitude and commitment to our *decision* to change. Think of your decision as a seed. You want to give your seed the best chance at life so you give it a great environment, lots of food and water, and after a few days your seed will begin to grow. This same thing happens when you make that small decision to change. At first, it may feel challenging, but keep watering your seed with new and improved language. Speak life over yourself and your dream. Speak abundance versus lack. Speak victory over failure and watch your garden grow.

We have all experienced deferred hopes and dreams that sometimes don't come true. Sometimes, success doesn't happen the way we think it should, but we can and should remain inspired. It took me 1,822 days to see the manifestation of the miraculous birth of my daughter. Don't give up on your dreams. In due season, you will reap if you don't faint.

The Blame Game

Nakikia A. Wilson, MHSA

*Do not conform to the pattern of this world, but be
transformed by the renewing of your mind.*
—Romans 12:2 (NIV)

REPEAT AFTER ME: No matter what, keep it moving.

I feel extremely confident in writing that many of us share
the belief that who we are, how we are, or why we are the
way that we are as adults has been shaped by our cul-
ture, our family dynamics, or the environment we were
raised in. I am pretty sure that many of us also share the
belief that these experiences have influenced the way we
see ourselves and how we perceive other people or the
world in general. I believe it is safe to say that our experiences have been the catalyst behind most our behaviors
and have shaped of our mentalities. Unfortunately, many
of the experiences in our family dynamics have not always produced or encouraged the healthy attitudes and
behaviors needed for mental wellness and emotional
security. Many of us have experienced and are products
of family dysfunction. What is more unfortunate is that
the perpetuation of dysfunction and toxicity in families
has resulted in children becoming toxic adults who are

mentally and emotionally broken, generation after generation.

The fact is that these same toxic attitudes and behaviors have proven to be the cause of my own self-sabotage, low self-esteem, limited beliefs, feelings of rejection, and the root of my need for validation and approval. I consistently engaged in unhealthy, toxic relationships. The toxic attitudes and behaviors I displayed were the result of the frustration of trying to fill voids or create a sense of comfort in my life. As a way to control and mask the pain from my negative experiences, I adopted negative attitudes and engaged in destructive behaviors that only temporarily distracted me from the discomfort and unpleasantries I believed were just a part of life.

There is this game I played, probably the same game many of you are playing right now. It's called the blame game. You know. The game where it's always something or someone else's fault, the finger is always pointed in the direction of something or somebody else, or there is a belief that everything or everyone else is wrong. It's the game that removes responsibility and accountability for the toxic behaviors and attitudes that we should be owning! Come on now! I know you know the game. The game you probably recently played with your husband or wife. You probably just played it with your girlfriend, boyfriend, or even on the job. Yeah, that game! I was good at this game. And I was winning too.

I blamed others for who I was, how I was, or why I was, especially when I experienced feelings of discomfort, negative emotions, and thoughts of perceived or real threats. It was always someone else's fault that I was in a bad mood. It was always someone else's fault that I was angry. I made other people responsible for the mistakes I made or the consequences of my dumb decisions. It was someone else's fault that I was overweight and the people I liked didn't like me. I blamed other people for my failures and unhappiness. I blamed everyone else for not liking the person I saw reflected in the mirror. I played this game with any and everybody. Er'body was an opponent. I didn't care who you were or where you came from. The type of relationship didn't matter either. My family, friends, co-workers, and even ex-partners have all been opponents in the blame game. What I never really understood at the time was why I was actually playing the game. What was the purpose? Was I even winning? Moreover, is the game ever worth playing?

Honey, allow me to provide the answers to those questions from the perspective of a person who was on both sides of the blame game. Let that marinate for just a moment. I know that last statement is probably leaving many of you in a state of utter confusion. It simply means that I have blamed others and I have been the one to blame for dysfunction. Okay, now that you're with me, I'll continue. The blame game, for me, was a type of defensive tactic used to maintain a facade of self-confidence or to hide the fact that I did not have a healthy amount of mental and emotional security. I did not understand how to love myself nor did I know my own worth. I, as so many others often do, played this game to support the great wall of protection I built around life to guard against the constant reminders of being overweight at a young age, the belief that my mom wasn't around because she didn't want to be in my life (thus, choosing a life of drugs for nearly three decades), and always being told I would be just like her by an alcoholic father and other family members who also supported the beliefs that I would be promiscuous, become a young mother, or choose a life of drugs.

I remember writing a letter to this guy when I was somewhere around the age of thirteen or fourteen. He was leaving for Job Corps. He was a bit older and, of course, he had some sexual experience. I really liked him a lot and I didn't want to seem juvenile (although, technically, I was). So, I wrote the letter using "adult language" and references to sexual activity. Honey, I was a straight virgin still and had never seen the likes of a boy's manhood. Okay! But the letter I wrote was darn near pornographic to convince him that I had sexual experience as well or that I, at least, had some level of maturity. I believed that would be the key to making him like me as much as I liked him. Well, he never received that nasty letter I had written. Instead, I folded the stupid thang up and naively hid it between the mattresses of the twin bed I slept in at my grandparent's house. If you haven't guessed by now, the letter was found by my grandma while she was changing the bed linen, and she made sure she gave it to my daddy! Lord have mercy! Chillleee. I just knew I was about to get beat dowwwnnn! But I didn't get beaten down physically; instead, I was emotionally defeated by feelings of shame, guilt, and the belief that I had validated their accusations about who I was and what I would become.

No matter what I did or said to make people proud of me or to get them to believe in me, it never seemed good enough or acceptable. So, I learned to play the blame game as a way of protecting myself from the constant criticism and lack of emotional support that came from trying to win the affection and approval of the adults I believed were supposed to love and protect me. Instead, as a young girl, I was left to suffer in silence and extreme loneliness. Rather than receiving mental and emotional security, I continued to be met with accusations of promiscuity or acting inappropriately simply because I desired to receive a hug or to hear the words "I love you" from the people who claimed they cared for me.

The object of the game was to make something or someone responsible for the negative feelings, thoughts, emotions, and toxic attitudes and behaviors learned as a result of the dysfunctional family environment I was brought up in. I did not learn or understand accountability. I learned to make excuses and place blame. The blame game allowed me to project and deflect just as the adults in my life had done. It allowed me, again, like the adults in my life had done, to excuse myself from bad behaviors or poorly made decisions, more specifically as I entered adulthood. The goal in this game of blame was to inflict pain or discomfort on any and everybody before they could inflict pain or discomfort on me. My guard was always up, even with those who came into my life unaware of the bags of trash I carried every day. They probably genuinely desired to show me love or compassion.

What I had failed to realize was that my engagement in the game of blame only added fuel to the already festering fires of the fragility of my mental and emotional stability. What I had not realized was that those same mental and emotional insecurities would spill over into every aspect of my life. As a result of my insecurities, I allowed my negative thoughts, feelings, and emotions to control how I responded to undesirable and unpleasant situations. I had no clue at the time how emotionally insecure and immature I was. I remember going home from college to Kinston, North Carolina, for the weekend. I found out that my then boyfriend had been unfaithful once again and had begun to see another woman. I allowed my emotions to control me. I went to the girl's house where he was at the time to confront him about his lies and deceit. I know! Lord knows I know now! It was a dumb move. Hey, I was young and dumb. Well, he got mad and pushed me. I beat his ass. By the time I arrived at my dad's house, a cop who knew me and my ex-boyfriend was waiting to arrest me for stalking and assault. I had to take that ride downtown in handcuffs. I remember crying and the cop saying, "I don't know what is going on, but I have a strong feeling it's something stupid and you shouldn't be riding in this car right now." Fast forward, my boyfriend dropped the charges and convinced me he loved me and wanted to be with me. I ended up taking the fool right back. Ugh, my daddy was pissed!

I internalized so many things even when they didn't concern nor have anything to do with me specifically. I was always on the defense, especially when I felt wronged in any way, shape, or form. Honey, this toxic behavior almost got me expelled from college after I tried to get into the Office of the Dean to curse out and put my foot in the ass of the secretary. For some unhealthy, irrational reason, I felt the heffa wronged me and I was about to handle her. I remember banging and kicking on the door, hoping and wishing someone would let me inside the building. However, there's a saying that "God protects babies and fools." As I continued my efforts to break the door down, I heard a familiar voice off in the distance calling my name in an effort to stop me from self-destructing. Somebody had gone and snitched on me to the one person who most times was able to snap me, the fool, back to reality. Thanks, Ms. Roseboro, I know I got on your nerves. You saved my college career though. Thank God! Nevertheless, I continued to move through life, even after those embarrassing actions, from a place of pain and victimization.

The blame game allowed me to avoid making positive behavioral changes or developing emotional maturity. It allowed me to withhold forgiveness and avoid working towards a resolution from my toxic and unhealthy family dysfunction. The blame game allowed me to use my wounds as excuses to behave in ways that have been unkind, unloving, or malicious towards family, friends, and other people I care about. The blame game, ultimately, left me in a dark and painful place with the wounds I have worn for so very long. I relinquished emotional control to fear, confusion, anger, misunderstanding, self-hate, and other insecurities as a result of the blame game. But one day, a lightbulb came on and revealed the truth. I started to see beyond my pain. I realized the essence of who I am and who I'm meant to be.

There is a saying that "You may not be the cause of your wounds, but you are responsible for your healing." I didn't write that saying, but for me it is very powerful.

This quote has put the ball in the court of my mind, body, and spirit. It is my responsibility to create and maintain a place of mental and emotional peace. It's up to me to use the pain from my life to promote mental health awareness, resolving family dysfunctions, and the understanding that healing starts on the other side of forgiveness. The wounds I wear are now in the healing process because I've chosen to take control of my life and take the necessary actions to become someone the Most High can use to be transparent and represent what it means and how it feels to experience healing on the other side of forgiveness.

My story is a clear example of what continues to happen when dysfunctions are never addressed or resolved but instead become normalized as a part of everyday life. My story is an example of why so many of us in communities of color suffer with mental health issues like anxiety, depression, and in many cases, PTSD. My family, like so many others, has perpetuated and enabled toxic and unhealthy behaviors and attitudes. The only attempt to address or discuss instances of family dysfunction was during periods of extreme negative emotions. Most of the time, those negative emotional experiences were provoked by insecurities often fueled by alcohol and drugs. There was a lot of displaced anger, finger pointing, or blaming of abusive and manipulative behaviors in my family dynamic. No one held themselves or anyone else accountable for avoiding, ignoring, denying, and continuing the family pathology. Unfortunately, I and many people around me were sorely impacted.

I had to unlearn negative attitudes and behaviors that encouraged denying, avoiding, and ignoring mental wellness and emotional security. I had to unlearn normalizing mental and emotional trauma, shame, and guilt. I have had to embrace the pain and allow myself to sit in negative feelings, thoughts, and emotions in order to start living in God's purpose for my life. I decided to take control by sitting in all of the negative feelings of rejection, abandonment, and worthlessness and forced myself to face the source and root of my pain. I had to work toward a resolution that would finally allow healing to take place in my life. I took back emotional control, no longer giving control to those responsible for the cause of my wounds.

I now acknowledge, accept, and have taken proper actions to ask for and extend forgiveness to the mentally and emotionally unhealthy fifteen-year-old mother and nineteen-year-old father who were ill-equipped to support me and provide me with a sense of security. I now acknowledge, accept, and have taken proper actions to extend and ask for forgiveness from the mentally and emotionally unhealthy family members who enabled toxic behaviors. I now extend forgiveness to those who did not have the capacity or understanding to teach me what it means to love myself properly. I extend forgiveness to myself for not knowing my worth or valuing myself. I now recognize my own mental and emotional triggers and the triggers fueled by the insecurities projected by or deflected from others. I hold myself and others accountable for negative attitudes or misbehaviors. I now have boundaries for myself and others who want to be a part of my healing journey.

I have had such a strong desire to put my *truth* and my story in the atmosphere and this is one of the many reasons I'm writing this chapter. For quite some time, I've been on a journey of forgiving and healing from past traumas and other negative experiences as it relates to generations of toxic attitudes and behaviors in my family. I've been on a personal journey of healing and experiencing a life of wholeness—mind, body, and spirit. Each day, I am growing and becoming more comfortable with expressing my authentic self. More and more, I am loving the person I am and who I am becoming. There has been a drastic change in how I see myself. There is also a significant change in what I believe about myself. I'm trusting myself more and more as I grow forward. Yes, it's been difficult, but I've continued to rise to the challenge of accepting, trusting, and loving myself. Even with all of the challenges of learning and embracing who I've become and who I'm yet to become, it has been invigorating and liberating at the same time. I've learned that many of the things I previously took to heart, believed, or thought about myself and others because of negative childhood experiences was severely distorted, unfair, and toxic. Those same perceptions and beliefs left me feeling devalued, unloved, angry, and ashamed. Because of that, throughout my life, I made everyone and everything responsible for my feelings and emotions. However, the things I've come to learn and accept about who I am, how I am, and why I am have enlightened me greatly. I have become eternally grateful for the journey and have embraced the process of healing in order to grow forward with each day I am blessed to see. More importantly, I have learned a very eye-opening concept on this journey—perception is not always reality.

"Owning our story and loving ourselves through that process is the bravest thing we'll ever do."
—Brené Brown

I own my story and appreciate all I've endured as it has been part of my healing process. I boldly and proudly acknowledge and accept the wounds I wear. I wear them in hopes of encouraging and inspiring others to start their own healing journey. I pray that others will *choose* healing. It's an absolutely amazing feeling to experience. I truly embrace and trust the process of being *healed*, and I'm dedicated to the work that needs to be done daily. With an open heart and mind, I continue to practice the art of mindfulness and love of self to achieve and maintain the healthy level of mental and emotional peace I know I deserve! I choose to release pain and live in a place of peace.

BEAUTIFULLY BROKEN

Tanisha Danielle

I know what I'm doing. I have it all planned out—
plans to take care of you, not abandon you,
plans to give you the future you hope for.
—Jeremiah 29:11 (MSG)

REPEAT AFTER ME: I will trust in the Lord with all my heart because I know, without a shadow of a doubt, God knows what He is doing. My faith is strong!

Sunlight streams through the slightly opened blinds. I can hear the birds chirping outside. Spring is here. The sun's rays illuminate the dark room and bounce off the chestnut mirrored dresser and onto the wooden bookcase. Despite the birds singing beautifully outside, in the corner curled up against the plush carpet, faint cries concealed by my blanket are heard. My cries become harder to hide. My world is caving in, and mentally it's overwhelming.

I've asked the Lord, "Why me?" What other questions were there to ask? Maybe, "How can you help me, God?" Then, not knowing where to start or who could help, I implored God's intervention. "God," I said, "I'm losing the battle."

Suddenly, that still, small voice on the inside of me said, "No, my child, you're winning the battle." That's the moment I realized I was being beautifully broken.

The Beginning

Before moving forward, let's define the words toxic and habit. The Merriam-Webster dictionary defines toxic as extremely harsh, malicious, or harmful. The word habit is defined as an acquired mode of behavior that becomes nearly or entirely uncontrollable. I would therefore define the phrase "toxic habits" as dangerous behavior that becomes uncontrollable. Unbeknownst to me, my toxic habits would take root before I reached my teenage years.

I began questioning myself in elementary school with the straightforward question, "Who am I?" I knew there was a missing piece to the puzzle. That missing piece was not knowing who my birth father was and not having a relationship with him. That's when the anger took root. Not knowing my birth father was the start of what I defined as toxic habits. Lashing out became the norm from elementary through high school. As time passed, my anger began to grow. I didn't know any other way but to act out, and before I knew it, the people who were closest to me and even the ones I had no association with had already labeled me. Some of the labels associated with me were rebellious, bad, unfriendly, bad-tempered, having attention-deficit disorder (ADD), and selfish. The devil had a plan for my life, and according to John 10:10, that plan was, and still is, to steal, kill, and destroy you and me.

The Labels

At a very early age, I questioned who I was. Not knowing who my father was and not having a relationship with him was a critical piece to the puzzle. That missing piece was the key and the answer to my question, "Who am I?" Or so I thought. What I did know about my birth father was that he had a long-standing battle with heroin. Yet, as I write this chapter, I am still unaware of his whereabouts.

When I questioned my identity, the enemy immediately began to go to work. I did not know, at the time, who I was or whose I was, so the adversary had a plan in motion. Remember John 10:10? The enemy comes to destroy. Stay with me, I'm going somewhere with this. I was unaware of who I was or whose I was, so I would accept the labels given to me by others. Before I go on, let me make mention that those labels were far from the truth. Today, I praise God because as Jeremiah 1:5 says, before I was formed in the womb, *He* knew me! Yes, *He knew me*! He had a plan for my life. That plan was to take care of me, not abandon me, and give me the future I would one day hope for. Yes, God knew me, but I did not know Him. Not only did I not know my birth father, but I did not know my heavenly Father. What I did know was what was being told to me by others. I accepted the truth of who I was because I did not have the missing piece of the puzzle at that time.

The Results of Not Knowing

I knew there was more to me than what I was being told or shown. Those closest to me misunderstood me at a very early age. When Satan comes to steal, kill, and destroy, he doesn't care who he uses to do it. So, after being admitted to a psychiatric hospital before I was even able to drive, something inside of me shifted. I felt helpless. But most of all, I felt hatred towards everyone.

I no longer felt anger. At the age of twelve, I felt hatred and unforgiveness. I was just a little girl from the inner city of Detroit wanting to know the answer to the question, "Who am I?" and the answer was inside. At just twelve years old, I hated my life. But most of all, the girl staring back at me in the mirror held depression and sadness in her young eyes. Unwillingly being admitted into a psychiatric hospital became a pivotal moment in my life. My innocence was taken away. The answer to the question, "Who am I?" no longer mattered. I wanted revenge. The people I trusted the most betrayed me. Hatred and unforgiveness slowly consumed me.

At the time, all I could think about was the sweet revenge I would have on everyone involved. I wanted vengeance, it was mine, and they were going to feel it. Now that I am older and wiser, that time in my life is what I would define as displaying toxic habits. Dangerous behavior that became uncontrollable took root.

Anger and revenge had me at odds with my family, accompanied by two abortions, followed by the birth of my daughter. Toxicity consumed my life. My relationships were unhealthy, and college was no longer in my future, so I dropped out. I held onto those labels given to me as a little girl and continued to live my life in a downward spiral. But I didn't care. My future was my revenge. Who was I hurting? My relationships continued to fail; they weren't meaningful. Finally, having given birth to another child followed by another abortion, alcohol became my escape.

I am sharing bits of my past with you today, not because I am proud, but because I pray that my story gives you hope that if God gave me beauty for ashes, He is faithful enough to do it for you. God knew you before you were a thought. His future for you is in place. He's just waiting for you to seek Him. Your future is bright.

The Mindset Shift

The Mayo Clinic defines mental health disorders as a wide range of mental health conditions—disorders that affect your mood, thinking, and behavior.

I was tired. I knew there had to be more to me than what the world had told me. I knew I was more than what those closest to me had shown me. If I was aware of those things, I could guarantee that the enemy knew it too. The enemy fought so hard to keep me from knowing who Tanisha was. I had been put through so many storms and tests at an early age that I was exhausted. And truthfully, I was ready to throw in that white flag. I wanted to give up, and I had.

My mental health had deteriorated. The enemy began to place thoughts of anger, revenge, suicide, depression, and rejection into my head. I was drained, and I didn't want to feel the pain anymore. I needed the pain to go away for good.

Again, I knew there was more to me than what I had been told or shown. Therefore, I could not give in. I knew I had to fight. I knew I had to win. I knew I had to know the answer to the question, "Who am I?" I was in a spiritual battle. The enemy couldn't take me out. He did not have God's permission; therefore, he needed me to carry out the task for him just as he needed Job to curse God, as well as God's permission to do physical harm to Job (see Job 1:11-12, NLT). I realized that I needed to shift my mindset. My life depended on it. My children's lives depended on it. Your life depended on it. Yes, *you*. This battle was much bigger than me.

Beautifully Broken

As I sat tearfully on the soft, tan carpeted bedroom floor at my mother's home, I slowly lifted my head from the blanket. My teary eyes focused on the blurred, wooden bookcase. The sun's rays illuminated Joyce Meyer's book, *Battlefield of the Mind*. I heard a gentle voice say, "Start here." There was a war raging in my mind, and Joyce Meyer's book would provide a wealth of information on how to win the battle with God's help. It was at that very moment when I was weak that I became strong. At that time, I did not know that I was regaining my strength in a different way.

As I mentioned earlier, it was that still, small voice on the inside that spoke to me and said, "No, my child, you're winning the battle." In 2 Corinthians 12:9, Jesus said, "My grace is all you need. My power works best in weakness." I was weak. I was tired. I had thrown in the towel. I was mentally at my lowest point in life. I wanted to die, but I didn't have the strength or the courage to perform the task. I was ready to give up on my life to be with Jesus. Therefore, I implored God to take my life. I just wanted to be with Him. I didn't know how to untangle my mind to live victoriously. I didn't have the self-confidence to start. I wanted freedom from my mental torment. I wanted out, and I was willing to die for that freedom. Yes, I am a born again believer. I knew if I had departed this earth, I would transition to be with the Father. That much I did know. I need you to under-stand the seriousness of mental health disorders. Mental illness is a real thing, just as cancer is a real thing. They both should be treated, or significant damage will occur. Jesus told us in John 10:10 that the thief's purpose is to steal and destroy, but there is more to that verse. Jesus stated that His purpose is for you and me to have a rich and satisfying life.

The Lesson

God knew me before I was formed in the womb of my mother. Let's pause for a moment to think about that. You and I were known to God before conception had the opportunity to take place. He knew me. He knew who I was, and now I was about to learn the answer I had longed for to the question, "Who am I?"

What I didn't know at that moment of my mental breakthrough was that I was surrendering my life, my will, and my way of doing things to God. I was ready to give up *me* for the freedom to be with *Him*. I believe that was why God led me to Joyce Meyer's book, *Battlefield of the Mind*. She teaches from the Word of God how to align your thoughts with God's thoughts. Doing so will ultimately bring freedom and peace.

Let me suggest that if you are struggling with depres-sion, unforgiveness, anger, anxiety, or any toxic habits, you should seek God's help. His power works best in our weakness. I knew God cared about me the moment I was introduced to Him. My bishop made sure that his congregation knew God's Word. But I hadn't comprehended how much God loved me at that point and time in my life. For me, I didn't want to be let down again. You may have similar feelings but allow me to offer some encouragement to you. God wants to help you. He cares for you. His Word says, "Cast your cares upon Him because He cares for you." God is love. Therefore, call on Him. He's not surprised by any of your toxic habits. He knew you before you were formed in the womb. If you haven't accepted Christ as your Lord and Savior, stop right now, and pray the prayer of salvation according to Romans 10:9-10. Confess with your mouth that Jesus is Lord and believe in your heart (not your head) that God raised Him from the dead and you will be saved. Yes, it's that simple! If you're born again but sin separated you from God, there is a prayer for that found in 1 John 1:9. "If we confess our sins, he is faithful and just and will forgive us our sins and purify us from all unrighteousness." In the words of my pastor, "Your future is bright!"

Now that you have accepted Jesus into your life or rededicated your life to Him, let me offer you five things to help you along this journey called life with Christ. The first thing that will help you along this journey with Christ is having a solid inner circle of God-fearing friends. Having a solid inner circle is important because iron sharpens iron. I enjoy watching documentaries on animals. I have learned from watching these TV documentaries that a lioness will wait patiently for its prey to wander off by itself before striking. The Bible warns in 1 Peter 5:8 to stay alert because the enemy walks about like a roaring lion seeking who he can devour. The enemy will come, but when you have a solid tribe, you will never have to fight the battle alone.

Secondly, stay focused. Dr. DeeDee Freeman teaches how to focus on the promise not the process in her book *Focus*. It is so easy to lose sight of where we are going when our focus is on the process. Let me say again that this is spiritual warfare. Satan's purpose is to steal, kill, and destroy. God's purpose is that we have a rich and satisfying life. I would be lying if I said this journey with Christ is going to be easy, it's not. But I would not be lying when I say that my worst days with Christ are better than my best days without Him. Remain focused on the promises of God and you will have victory. It's a fixed fight, and you already won!

The third thing that will help you on this journey with Christ is speaking life over your mind. Remember that words are powerful. God created the earth with His words. It is said that where you are today is because of what you spoke yesterday. La'Ticia Nicole named her ministry Speak Life. She understands the assignment, and so should you. The Bible teaches us to encourage ourselves. Create affirmations and recite them through-out the day. I affirm every day that I have the mind of Christ, I will not return to that dark place, and I am confi-dent and courageous. I know my worth. I know who I am, and, more importantly, whose I am. I am a child of God, and I have a purpose to fulfill. It's that simple. I can share my past journey without guilt, shame, or condemnation because these five steps helped me.

This fourth step is essential. God can do all things, but He is also a gentle giant. He will meet you where you are. With that being said, it's okay to seek profes-sional counseling. Mental health is an illness. For some people, if not most, it requires professional counseling. This counseling would be with a trained professional that specializes in mental health disorders. If you were to break a leg, you would visit the nearest hospital emer-gency room for treatment. The same should be said for mental health. It's okay to seek a therapist.

Lastly, *breathe*! There will be times when it seems like steps one through four aren't working. That is when you should sit quietly, take a deep breath, exhale, and praise Him. God inhabits the praises of His people. You got this. You can do it. I am rooting for you!

The Settling of the Sacrificial Lamb

Shana Monique Williams

"For I know the plans I have for you," declares the Lord,
"plans to prosper you and not to harm you, plans to
give you a hope and a future."
—Jeremiah 29:11

REPEAT AFTER ME: I am who God says I am.

"Don't dim your light and stop settling to protect others!" Those were the words of my grandmother, also known as Grand Dolly. She always said I was too nice, too soft, and one day I would understand how important it was to stop being soft and catering to everyone except myself. I always told her she was wrong, and I could stand on my own and be my own woman. No one was going to put out my light. I would never settle for less. I never understood what she meant until I became an adult, a wife, a mother, and a daughter caring for her family.

Life for me seemed easy and I always did everything well. My parents were a great team; they loved me with everything, and I knew it. My sister and I were very close, and she was my number-one fan. Many things such as processing my future, what I was going to be doing ten years after high school, and what type of family I desired to care for went through my mind. I was always known as a nice person that would give you my last or just be a listening ear. I valued friendships and relationships, and I loved my family.

During my senior year of high school everything changed. In March 1998, I lost myself and my trust, and I gained some harsh lessons. Negativity overcame my mind along with suicidal thoughts. I began to worry about others' perception of me and the vibe I gave off. One violation of my self-esteem led to depression, anxiety, and constant questioning of myself. That cycle led me down a path of destruction where I felt like God did not hear me. I did not feel Him at all in my life. I became sad, angry, and lost. My faith was gone, and I could not go to church. Life had become difficult, and the path of destruction was dark. My depression and isolation led to the toxic behaviors of settling and sacrificing myself. Never had I cried so hard in my life than after the sexual assault that God allowed. Hmm, what a thought, huh?

Many do not understand how a sexual assault changes you. It strips every piece of strength you have. You lose your self-worth and your self-esteem, and you start to question every decision you make after that one hour of a man penetrating you and stealing your soul. You never really feel protected and free to open up to anyone ever again. You turn inward and your trust in people changes. You question your own state of mind and others question yours. Sexual assault makes you feel like you did something wrong. You feel dirty and judged. Your niceness turns into anger and then you start to think that maybe your light was too bright. Maybe you should do more to make sure that no one wants to hurt you ever again, especially when you have a son and later give up your parental rights to make sure that he will have a great life. My dark season became a season of loneliness, codependency, and settling for any expressions of love that came my way.

I wrote a lot to God within the first year of "the dark season of 1998-1999." I wrote to God about my son (who had been adopted), my state of mind, and who I met. Daily, I had to get my thoughts on paper so that God could understand where my heart and mind were. I consistently questioned why God had my son with another family and not me. Why could I not share that I had a son when I was sexually assaulted by one of our friends? Why could I not rely on my friends to help me with one of the hardest times in my life? Why was I so paranoid? Life was not fair! Nothing was helping me, and I missed how happy I was before March 1998. From October 1998 to January 1999, my path was dark; I was alone and damaged. I eventually stopped talking to God and the days of sacrifice became my reality.

My first day of settling came when I decided not to go back to the college I was attending prior to the birth of my son. Instead, I stayed home with my parents and attended college closer to home. I did not see myself as being strong enough to leave. I was not resilient, and I was not sure of any decisions. But college was the right thing to do, and it was a part of me thinking about my future. So, settling for that school checked the box.

The college years of 1999–2001 were about figuring out what I wanted as my goal of becoming a doctor had changed to becoming a nurse practitioner. I did everything from going to the library in between classes, to pledging, and finally going to internships at the one college I dreamed of graduating from as a nurse. As I accomplished each goal, I felt like my life was still not complete. I was not sure what kind of person I wanted to be or what career path I wanted to take. God had been sustaining me and keeping me sane, but I still did not feel Him. Yet, I kept writing and pushing for more, for greater.

From 2002–2005, I struggled to find my purpose, to recreate my relationship with God, and to juggle my many roles—daughter, sister, niece, cousin, grand-daughter, student, and nurse. My light was coming on as I achieved various goals within those roles. I became someone's girlfriend and I had goals again. I prayed, I cried, and I hoped that God was starting to hear me.

Yet, no matter how much I settled for all the lessons and blessings that were being dropped into my life, I had no peace. I had to continue to sacrifice to make sure that everything and everyone was taken care of. It gave me purpose to know that I mattered, and my life was worth something. Because of my sacrifice, I would be appreciated and valued. Everyone would see me and see how soft, gentle, and meek I was under my tough exterior. My dark path was still hard and long. My faith in God was gone even though I was attending church. I was starting to give up again and it did not matter who was in my life or what great things I was doing in my now ministry of nursing.

The day that I knew God heard me and I felt Him was June 15, 2006. My son's adoptive mother found me. She told me all about him and asked if I wanted to meet him. I could have only attributed the phone call to God deciding to show me who He is, yet I still lacked full trust in Him. Meeting my son brought me some peace, but I still saw settling and sacrificing as a way to feel better and get my light to come on.

From 2007–2009, I attempted to get back to myself and turn my light on. I faced many obstacles in both my personal and professional relationships. I wanted more blessings, yet I had many disappointments. The year 2009 was especially hard because I lost two important ladies that kept my dim light on and often reminded me of how far I had come. They were gone and once again I was angry with God and stepped back from Him. I also allowed situations to make my path so dark that I was sad when I should have been happy, I was lonely when I was in the presence of many, and I settled by marrying someone when I should have walked away. Life was once again unfair but those were the cards I was dealt, so I was going to play the hand.

I struggled again to find myself from 2010–2013. I wrestled with grief and nightmares again of the sexual assault. I fought to trust others and make a life and family with my husband in our new state. I was not happy; I was just going through the motions. I said to myself, *If I can make my home happy for him despite my emotions and his ways of protecting me, maybe I can get my light on. Maybe everyone in this new state and new church will like me.* I did not fit in, and I felt like a square peg in a round hole. I was going through the motions, unprepared for the greatest blessing that came next.

On February 26, 2013, my second son was born, yet I had never felt so lost and alone. I fasted and prayed to be a better mother to him than I was to my oldest son. I also realized while falling in love with my youngest son, my "Kingdom Kid," that I did not love myself. I did not have an idea of who I was and once again I did not know my life's purpose. My husband could not help me, and he was feeling alone. I had to push my feelings away and make sure that everyone else was okay, but now my path had become a rabbit hole.

From 2014–2018, I worked and took care of my home both financially and physically, but I was not adjusting to my new role as a mother. Spiritually, I was defeated. Several themes came out of those years:

One: I was not living the life I wanted to live. I felt like I had no say-so as others did not trust me to make my own decisions.

Two: I was missing feeling loved and being happy.

Three: I missed my day one friends, and I desired to have them back. I had stepped away to respect my marriage and the life I had built in another state.

Four: I was so nice and soft that everyone pulled on me.

Five: I was not learning from my past decisions.

Six: I was working a lot because to me that is what a woman does for her home. She sacrifices to make sure that her family is taken care of. (My independence was instilled in me by my father.)

Seven: My life had become routine, and I missed my roots. I had no identity.

From 2018–2021, I decided to take my life back and under no circumstances was I going to be stopped. That meant that I would review my whole life, and I was going to be under construction. Everyone was up for evaluations. And if they did not meet certain benchmarks, their time in my life would be terminated. But this time, I allowed God to show me the way. The rabbit hole was less deep, and God had provided the ladder to climb out of it. Climbing out of the rabbit hole meant facing fear, doubt, abandonment, rejection, and anger from all directions. God isolated me and removed people, places, and things. He and I became closer, and He held my hand. He put this prayer in my spirit: "God, You are my force and my life. It is in You that I trust. Fill me with Your Spirit. Fill me, Lord, with Your Spirit. I need it. I thank You for directing my path. I thank You for elevation. I thank You for taking me to my destiny. I thank You for the next level that You have prepared for me and my sons. Remove anyone that is not of You. I thank You that You will supply all I, my sons, my grandson, my daughter-in-love, my parents, my sisters, and my family can ever ask for."

A new story was forming, and it started like this:

Once upon a time, a woman had a big heart, and she gave. She gave of herself, and everyone liked her. One day, a friend damaged her big heart and she turned inward. She also gave a piece of her heart to her son she hoped to see again. She wanted to embrace everyone, so she loved and gave love. She met many men, but one man changed her heart. She married that man, and they had a son. The woman thought she had everything she ever wanted—a supportive husband and a family. She thought they were going to be unbreakable. At times, she felt lost within herself and her life, and she felt distant from God. One day, devastation struck her family and the man left. The woman struggled to understand what happened to her identity and to find peace. Then, more devastation struck, and the love of her life had a heart attack. She stopped everything to care for him, yet the heartbreak remained. She forgave him and he violated her trust and loyalty. She sought again to find her peace, her identity, and her light. She remembered the words Grand Dolly, Aunt Marilyn, and Aunt Jane said to her about how bright a light can shine on any dark path, but God must walk beside you. "Allow Him to direct your path," Aunt Dot would say. "God is always with you," her mother would say. "Write down your plans and make it plain," her sister would say. "Keep moving forward," Carlton and Kim would say. "Nothing good comes easy," her father would say. "You can't stop me now," her sons would say. The woman gained strength. She began to reach out to her tribe and reconnected with her day ones. She focused on her peace and happiness. She decided to be intentional and strategic. She had to get back to being the Proverbs 31 woman that aligned her priorities with God's priorities. She had to focus on loving those who loved and appreciated her. But she also had to learn how to love herself and embrace the beauty she had locked away that made her stunning on the inside and the outside. She had to fix her mouth and her face and take the time to nurture herself.

Her story will now end like this:

The woman has found her light and her peace. She keeps pushing forward towards healing, knowing who she is, and determining how she can impact many others. She allowed God to show her that He is pushing her to her next level, and she trusts Him. She now has a tribe that stood with her in the heat of a battle. She is unapologetic and open to loving someone that God will find for her. Her big heart, although misunderstood at times, remains intact and she can see the light. The rabbit hole is not deep at all, and she is on the path to even more greatness than she can imagine. While she and God have a relationship with up and downs, highs and lows, and thoughts that are hard to process, together they ride the wave to victory, blessings, and love. Her light shines bright every day, her life has meaning, and she is no longer the sacrificial lamb. Every one of her encounters has a new meaning, every Scripture has a totally different feeling, and every day is another day in which she celebrates and embraces her wonderful life!

Anxiety: The Power to Start with Self-Healing

Laurine S. Garner

Say to them that are of a fearful heart,
Be strong, fear not: behold, your God will
come with vengeance, even God with a recompense;
he will come and save you.
—Isaiah 35:4 (KJV)

REPEAT AFTER ME: Anxiety cannot run my life. I will not let that happen. Anxiety, you will not win.

There are several reasons I ended up in my current state of mind. I truly believe it started in my teenage life. As a child, I did not know I was living a shielded life from nearly all mishaps that could have been learning experiences. I thought I enjoyed my childhood, but as I grew older, I sensed something was wrong. I do not blame my parents for protecting us, but for merely not easing the grip just a little so that we would not be so confused or lost when we got out in public or on our own.

Becoming a teenager had its ups and downs. I was learning how to get around on my own. The problem was that no one taught me how to protect myself from those who meant me harm. After being snatched from the bus stop on my way to the dentist one day, I no longer wanted the freedom I thought I was beginning to receive. That happened on a Saturday morning. I was standing alone, waiting for the bus to go to the dentist when a man walked by me. I spoke; he spoke. I never looked behind me to see where he went. I felt as though he was a friendly person, so I did not have to check. To my surprise, someone grabbed me from behind. He wrapped his arms around my neck and pointed a knife at me. The sleeves were the same as those on the coat of the man that had recently spoken to me. I was terrified. He dragged me down an alley to a vacant house. I could see a lady looking out of her house window directly across the street from the bus stop. She offered no help. I was crying and afraid to fight for fear that he would stab me. As he got me inside of the house, he told me not to scream or he would kill me and take my clothes off. I was too young to understand what his intentions were. The thought of being alone with this stranger was terrifying. It was cold so I asked him why I should take my clothes off. After all, I was only thirteen years old. Back in my youthful days, thirteen-year-olds were still playing with dolls and toys. We were allowed to be playful children for as long as possible. I have never followed directions very well, unless I wanted to, and it paid off that time.

I screamed. As I was crying, the man ran to the window to see if anyone had heard me. I saw a peek of the sun shining through the boarded-up door. I ran to it, pried my fingers through the holes, and snatched the door open. I took off running very fast. It felt more like I was flying because I do not remember my feet ever touching the ground. I ran until I got to familiar territory—the home of a friend who went to the same school I did. They called the police and my parents. I still wonder if the police ever picked the man up. I am just pleased my father did not find him because it would not have turned out well for either of them.

After that ordeal, I became very sheltered and shameful. I believed it was my fault that the man attacked me. Although my clothes were not revealing any of my body parts, I felt the man must have thought that I was older than I was. Out of fear, I started wearing sweaters that covered my breasts (even in the heat of the summer) and shirts that covered my bottom. I was afraid of men. I did not trust any man outside of my family members. I am almost sure that is why I stay so close to them to this day. I feel that they are my protectors. I pray that none of them ever come at me in an abusive or sexual way. I have heard stories from back in the day about some of our family members, and they are genuinely traumatizing. I am so thankful for the type of father I had. I genuinely believe he is why none of that stuff ever happened to my sister and me within the family; him and the grace of God. The anxiety I get from thinking about what this unknown person did to me resides deep inside of me, searching for a way out.

Let's move on to my high school years. I loved my high school. The people there were like family and very close friends. But there are a few who almost ruined that family like feeling for me. Those few people must have felt like they were untouchable. I'm sure it was because their chests were stuck out too far with pride because of who they were. Maybe they felt like someone owed them something. I say this because a few members of the basketball team became aggressive with me. They took me upstairs to an area that looked like an old auditorium; it had been unused for several years. I can still remember the old purple-looking stage curtains hanging in my peripheral vision. One student in particular attempted to take my clothes off.

I did not realize what was going on. I did not understand that the guys were trying to rape me, mainly because I was still a virgin. I finally fought enough to get away from them. They were also startled by the sound of someone approaching to find out what the noise was. I escaped down another stairway. Out of fear, I never told anyone what happened. I recently talked to my best friend about it. If I had only known then to tell someone, I probably would not be full of anxiety now. To this day, I still hold some anger against the individual who attempted to take off my clothes. It is taking some work, but I am honestly trying to let it go. Even though the school no longer exists, we still have an annual all year's picnic, and it never fails to end with plenty of love and memorable smiles on our faces. Even though fun times are had by all, the anxiety I get when the main initiator of that incident shows up still resides deep inside of me, searching for a way out.

My military years had their ups and downs. Though I am happy and proud of the years I served, I experienced several downfalls while I was enlisted. I will skip a few mishaps on purpose, as sharing them might ruin the relationships I have with several people that may come across this book. Reflecting on my second tour, my first tour overseas, I encountered an arrogant platoon sergeant. It was to the point that no one would take him down for anything. My first few days there, he told me everything about myself. I started to believe that it was normal for the leaders to know everything about up-and-coming soldiers as they arrived on a military base. Every day after that, he seemed to growl at the entire platoon. He would curl his nose up at us as though we disgusted him. In his eyes, we were beneath him.

One Saturday morning, I was headed to the shuttle bus to go shopping. It seemed as though everyone else was already gone for the day, maybe even the weekend.

As I approached the door, my platoon sergeant was there. I stepped to the side to let him in. The sergeant kept dancing in front of me. That fiasco went on for several seconds. When I finally just stood there, he grabbed my breasts. I told him to remove his hands while I tried to pry them away. He was a husky man, so all I could do was wrestle with him until he finally released me. As he did, he said, "You know this is called sexual harassment, don't you?" I said, "Yes, I do, and I'm going to report you to the authorities." He did not care. He turned around and left with a smirk on his face. I had not made many friends during that time, so the only person I could talk to was my roommate. She, too, became upset and encouraged me to tell someone about it.

On Monday morning, I reported the incident to a higher-ranking official. There was a meeting held where my platoon sergeant and I were summoned to appear in front of a board simultaneously. The committee questioned both of us, and we both gave truthful answers. My platoon sergeant admitted everything he did while looking as though he didn't have a care in the world. The board decided to place him in charge of another platoon. Two weeks later, they put him back in control of my platoon, disregarding my fears. For the next few months, he continued to verbally harass me. He also gave me horrifying looks, extra uncalled-for demands of details, and duties that made life very uncomfortable for me.

Of course, I was angry with the way things turned out, but what could I do? Half of the platoon and board were mad at me for telling on him, while the other half told me I did the right thing. I believe I did what was right for me. The drama continued until he departed from overseas. I had nearly reached a point where I did not trust any man. Once again, the anxiety I get from just the thought of this person resides deep inside of me, searching for a way out.

After that ordeal, I decided to End Term of Service (ETS) from active duty in the Army; however, during my ETS process, I decided I did not want to get out. I asked an out-processing captain if I could go back to active status. He reviewed my records and said yes, I could. I decided to change jobs, so I ended up going to school to learn my new job. The first day there, I met a few people. I remember a girl we called Jamaica because that was her nationality. She and her accent were beautiful. She was from London, England. Jamaica and I were best buddies, but we lost touch over the years. Another person I met was a rather strange guy whose name I won't reveal, but they called him, let's say, Robo Man. The reason they called him that was because he seemed to believe that he could do the robot dance with perfection like no other. If only you could see my eyes rolling. He somehow became infatuated with me on my first day there. As we sat in the bleachers listening to the lecture that was taking place, a bumblebee kept flying around the platoon, and Robo Man decided to catch it. He tried and tried and finally had it in his hand. Robo Man began dissecting the bee, piece by piece. One leg at a time, he ate it. I don't know what he did with the body because I got up from my seat and moved as far away from him as possible. That act put a seal on what most of us believed about him seeming to be very strange.

On the weekends, we were all allotted passes to leave the post. I had begun sheltering myself from those I did not know. I did so because of prior incidents. So, while the others would visit nearby family or go shopping, I always got a room at the nearby hotel away from everyone. That was my comfort zone, my space. After a couple of weeks of going to the hotel, I became comfortable with that routine. One day, someone kicked in my hotel room door. I jumped up out of fear only to realize that it was Robo Man. I thought, *What does he want? Why would he kick in the door instead of knocking?* I was terrified. He started walking towards me. When I got ready to scream, he told me that I had better not holler or I would be sorry I did. To my surprise, he slapped me twice so hard I saw stars. I started crying. No one had ever smacked me before. I was in total shock. He snatched me up off the floor, where I'd fallen when he hit me, and threw me on the bed. He ripped my gown and panties off and began to force himself onto me. I could not believe this was happening yet again. When he finished, he fixed himself up like nothing ever happened and pointed in my face and said, "You better not tell a soul. If you do, I will kill you." He continued, "I will follow you here every weekend, and you better not ever have nobody else in here with you."

I was scared for my life. I stopped going to the hotel, but that did not stop Robo Man from coming to my room. He always waited for my roommate to leave for the night or weekend. He continued to do that for several months. The very last time it happened, he brought three of his friends with him. I only remember one guy's last name and I also remember that one of the other guys was married. While Robo Man held a weapon to my head, the three other men ran a train on me and made me perform oral and anal sex against my will. I was afraid to move because of the weapon, so all I could do was cry. I cried that entire weekend, and I did not tell a soul because I was horrified. I nearly developed social anxiety disorder. According to the Mayo Clinic, "in social anxiety disorder, also called social phobia, everyday interactions cause significant anxiety, self-consciousness and embarrassment because you fear being scrutinized or judged negatively by others." Yet again, the anxiety I get from those men sexually assaulting me resides deep inside of me, searching for a way out.

Anxiety, you do not win. According to Medical News Today, "When an individual faces potentially harmful or worrying triggers, feelings of anxiety are not only normal but necessary for survival." Working through anxiety is indeed a process, and every person deals with it differently. I had to begin with self-love, which I am still working on to this day. I never believed I was beautiful; I thought I looked like a bullfrog. I was told that constantly as a little girl. I wondered why all of those men treated me the way they did. Is that how men treat women who do not feel beautiful and show a lack of confidence in themselves? Do I show a lack of confidence in myself? Is that written on my forehead, or do I show it in the way I carry myself? Regardless, I am still fighting internally. I eventually had to seek medical attention.

I ended up getting help from a therapist, a social worker, and a chaplain, all of whom gave me their undivided attention. I requested a non-male team. But to work on easing my trust issues, I agreed to a male chaplain, as long as my appointments are virtual. He started by reading me a Scripture from Psalms to calm my anxiety. It read, "Do not be anxious about anything, but in every situation, by prayer and petition, with thanksgiving, present your requests to God."—Philippians 4:6 (NIV). I am working on my people skills. Don't get me wrong, I am very friendly, but I am also very cautious about the people I talk to. If I do not feel safe, I will go into my shell just like a snail. With self-love, I make myself feel pretty as best I can. I put on all of my jewelry—my earrings, necklace, watch, and bracelets. I am a perfume and a shoe fanatic. I cannot leave home without either. My perfume must smell good enough to get compliments, and my shoes must match whatever I have on.

It was not easy for me to talk to anyone about my anxiety issues, but it was truly a relief when I finally did. I am always smiling, so no one ever knew what I was going through unless I mentioned it. I have forgiven those men with whom I never had a personal relationship. I did that for myself. I have also forgiven those I did not mention, whom I once dated. We will save them for another time. I am determined to live my life fear free. I have to start somewhere. Because I have taken the step to forgive those who I believe have done me wrong, now it is time to forgive myself. I need to forgive myself for doubting that I could have been more than I set out to be. I know God will see me through and allow me to build on the things I have put off because of my fears. The accomplishment will be visible to everyone.

My dream is to build a foundation that will help people who have gone through the same traumatic experiences I have been through. I do not want any other woman to tolerate those cruel experiences unless it is their desire to do so. But I honestly refuse to believe that anyone wants that type of treatment. If you think you do, seek help. Talk to someone. It is best to talk to a profes-sional rather than talking to someone you know. I say this because the people you know may be judgmental. They could also be someone you thought you could trust with confidential information, only to find out they were never the ones to be trusted. We do not need personal opin-ions; we need someone to listen. I said it before, and I find much pleasure in saying it again: "Anxiety, you do not win."

About the Authors

Katrina Bridges was born in San Diego, California, and raised in the St. Louis metro area where she currently works and resides. With a strong drive to succeed and a worth ethic that often goes unmatched, Katrina worked diligently on her education. She received a bachelor of science in organizational leadership, a master of science in management practice from Greenville University in Illinois, and a master of business administration from Missouri Baptist University.

Katrina utilizes her degrees as a part of the executive staff for an online travel and marketing organization. She is also an entrepreneur, earning income through several streams including business management consulting and analytical business reviews.

While Katrina has accomplished much in her short career and at a young age, she is most proud of her three children—Marcus, Aaliyah, and Kaden—whom she adores.

Katrina's personal mission statement is: "I encourage and motivate others to believe that anything they desire can happen."

To connect, email her at katrinabridges31@gmail.com

La'Ticia Nicole Beatty, RN, BSN, MBA, a native of Detroit, Michigan, is a certified life coach, motivational speaker, nursing home administrator, and the bestselling author of seven books including *Healing Toxic Habits, I am Beautiful, SpeakLife: 90-Day Devotional, and Unsilenced Faces of Domestic Violence.* She is also the founder of Purposed Professionals Inc.; Laticia Nicole Enterprise, LLC; Speak Life Transformational Institute; an independent vitamin and herbal tea company owner; and chief editor of *Speak Life Magazine.*

La'Ticia established Speak Life Enterprises to serve women and girls who feel stuck because of fear, rejection, depression, mental illness, or post-traumatic syndrome. Known as the Transformation Evangelist, La'Ticia electrifies audiences around the world. She is a child of the Almighty God and is on a mission to encourage and transform people out of dead situations through #Speaklife Enterprises.

La'Ticia has been married to her husband, Antonio, for nearly twenty years. They have two children, one cat, and reside in Durham, North Carolina.

Learn more at www.laticianicole.com

Trish Noel Patricia "Trish" Noel has a heart for those with no voice, which inspired her to become a licensed clinical social worker associate, a licensed clinical addiction specialist associate, a North Carolina certified forensic evaluator, and a certified life coach. During the height of the COVID-19 pandemic, she became the CEO and founder of Noel Integrated Services, Incorporated (NIS), which provides mental health and substance use services to individuals, children, families, couples, and groups. Out of NIS was born Just Breathe, a support group for females ages twelve to nineteen struggling with anxiety, depression, self-harm, and suicidal ideations.

Trish is originally from Baltimore, Maryland, and has resided in Durham, North Carolina, since 2010. She is the mother of three, a parental caregiver, and a "mom" to the family doggie, Tzu Tzu. She enjoys cooking, watching the Food Network, traveling, and hosting family and friends.

To connect, email her at NIServInc@gmail.com

Yolanda Spearman has a reputation that stems from the commercials we hear on television. She is a sales trainer by day and a voice talent, known as the Voiceover Lady, by night. She earned an MBA from Clark Atlanta University, studied art in Paris, France, and is from Detroit, Michigan.

Yolanda is the proud mother of two and resides in a Michigan suburb with her husband and family. Peppered throughout her successful careers are awards, accolades, and certificates for her ability to teach, train, and sell. Yolanda's fascinating career journey led her from a first-grade classroom in the Detroit Public School System, to Ford Motor Company, then to Harley-Davidson Financial Services, and now she is a voiceover talent and author of the book *Relentless Execution*. Her exuberant personality marks everything she does.

Yolanda is on a mission to help people on their joy journey. Her motto is: "Do what makes you happy and live a life without regrets."

To connect, email her at
yolanda@yolandavo.com

Nakikia A. Wilson, MHSA, aka CoachKeepItMoving, is a graduate of Winston-Salem State University where she earned a bachelor's in radio and television. After several years in the television industry, Nakikia realized her passion was in advocacy and completed the health services administration master's program at Strayer University.

Dedicated to normalizing and advocating for mental and emotional health in communities of color, she shares her personal health experiences regarding living with mental and emotional health challenges and combating multiple sclerosis. Nakikia's mental health advocacy has been featured in such publications as *STS Branding and Publishing Magazine and Where It All Began*, as well as a multitude of podcasts, radio shows, and streaming platforms.

Nakikia is the owner of KIMCESS, LLC and Founder of K.I.M. (Keep It Moving) 4U, Inc. She holds several certifications as an emotional intelligence practitioner, life and emotional support coach, mental health awareness advocate, and most recently, adult and youth mental health first aid.

Learn more at www.KIMCESS.com

Tanisha Danielle received her bachelor of business administration with a concertation in marketing from Baker College. She has experience helping small and mid-sized businesses grow. Tanisha is a volunteer within the nonprofit, faith-based sector, specializing in social media, TV production, and children's church ministry. In addition, she sits on the board of directors for a nonprofit youth assistance program that strengthens youth and the family unit.

Tanisha knew her purpose early in life, but guilt and shame from her past and the fear of being rejected prevented her from walking in it. Now that she understands the importance of walking in one's purpose, Tanisha is dedicated to helping women discover their purpose and go after it with passion while pursing God. For this reason, Stronger Within, an organization set to help women with purpose and passion who are in pursuit of God, was birthed.

To connect, email her at
Strongerwithin2020@gmail.com

Shana Monique Williams is a Charleston, South Carolina, native. Shana loves being a nurse and doctoral prepared psychiatric nurse practitioner. She is passionate about the care and engagement of those experiencing behavioral health illnesses and is a part of a collaborative team that is impacting the future of the nursing profession.

Shana currently lives in Durham, North Carolina, with her two sons: Christopher John and Shane. She enjoys spending time with the love of her life and her family, fellowshipping with friends, reading, watching movies, and taking walks in the park. She is kind of a fun nerd.

Shana loves people and makes sure that everyone she comes in contact with has the best life. Her philosophy is: "God has given me the best part of life and it is just the beginning."

To connect, email her at
docshamonique@gmail.com

Laurine S. Garner is from Detroit, Michigan. She is the mother of three wonderful sons, two thirty-three-year-olds and one twenty-nine-year-old. She also has four beautiful grandchildren, two girls ages thirteen and nine, and two boys ages fourteen and two. Laurine is a proud Veteran of the United States Army, in which she served for eight years. Her status is combat Veteran.

Laurine has both a bachelor's and a master's degree in business administration, and a second master's degree in occupational safety and health. She has been at her current place of employment for twenty-eight years, with nineteen and a half of those years as a health and safety representative, graduate safety practitioner (GSP).

Despite all of the wonderful things in her life, anxiety still plays a significant role in Laurine's past and present. Her current goal is to help others conquer this roadblock and move forward with their lives. Her current status is panic level anxiety.

To connect, email her at laurinegarner@gmail.com

Endnotes

1 Mayo Clinic. "Mental Illness." Accessed October 28, 2021.https://wwwmayoclinic.org/diseases-conditions/ mental-illness/symptoms-causes/syc-20374968#:~:- text=Mental%20illness%2C%20also%20called%20 mental,eating%20disorders%20and%20addictive%20 behaviors.

2 Mayo Clinic. "Social anxiety disorder (social phobia)." Accessed October 28, 2021. https://www.mayoclinic. org/diseases-conditions/social-anxiety-disorder/ symptoms-causes/syc-20353561.

3 *Medical News Today*. "What to Know About Anxiety." Accessed October 28, 2021. https://www.medical- newstoday.com/articles/323454.

CREATING DISTINCTIVE BOOKS
WITH INTENTIONAL RESULTS

We're a collaborative group of creative masterminds
with a mission to produce high-quality books to position
you for monumental success in the marketplace.

Our professional team of writers, editors, designers,
and marketing strategists work closely together to ensure
that every detail of your book is a clear representation
of the message in your writing.

Want to know more?
Write to us at info@publishyourgift.com
or call (888) 949-6228

Discover great books, exclusive offers, and more at
www.PublishYourGift.com

Connect with us on social media

@publishyourgift

CPSIA information can be obtained
at www.ICGtesting.com
Printed in the USA
BVHW050259040522
635996BV00046B/4451

9 781644 845608